Collins Primary Science

THINGS CHANGE

Linda Howe

Acknowledgements

Copyright © 1991 Linda Howe
ISBN 0 00 317587 1
Published by Collins Educational an imprint of
HarperCollins *Publishers*, London and Glasgow

Design by Shireen Nathoo
Illustrations by Sally Neave, Gay Galsworthy,
Belinda Evans (The Gallery)
Cover illustration by Debi Ani
Commissioned photography by Chris Gilbert

Typeset by Kalligraphic Design Ltd., Horley, Surrey
Printed and bound in Hong Kong

The publishers thank Fielding Middle School, London
and Woolpit County Primary School, Suffolk for their kind
co-operation in the production of Collins Primary Science.

Photographs - The publishers would like to thank the
following for permission to reproduce photographs:

Barnaby's Picture Library 10(t), 30(tc), 38(x2),
J Allan Cash Photolibrary 11, 30(tl) (tr), 38(x3)
Robert Harding Picture Library 41

t = top, b = bottom, c = centre, l = left, r = right

Contents

HELPFUL NOTES

In these books you will be:

★ trying out ideas

★ seeing what you can find out

★ making and using models

★ using different ways to show what you find out

Look out for these signs and they will help you.

This sign is at the beginning of each activity.
The activities give you ideas for things you can make, things you can try and ways of finding things out.

This sign tells you what you need to collect before you begin an activity. Things that you might need are shown in the box. If you can't find all the things in the list think of other things in your classroom that you could use instead. Remember that we just give you ideas for materials to use. You may need to find other things so that you can try out your own ideas.

This sign asks you to think of ideas of your own. Always talk your ideas over with a friend as they can usually help you with your thinking.
Before you try a test of your own, plan it carefully.
Remember these things:

1. Think about what you want to make, try, or find out.

2. Collect what you need.

3. Try out your ideas. Can you improve them in any way?

4. Record what you have done.

It is important to work safely and carefully.
Sometimes, when you are using tools or handling hot things, you will need to take special care.
This sign tells you when to take extra care.

When you see this sign you will need to find things out for yourself.
You will need to decide how to find out what you need. You may need to:

▶ look in some books from the library

▶ write some letters

▶ ask other people

▶ look closely at some pictures, the television or a video.

RECORD

When you are doing an activity you will need to think about how you will show what you find out. Sometimes you will need to choose a way that will help you remember what you have done and sometimes you will need to choose a way that will tell other people what you have found out. There are lots of ways of recording your activities. Here are some for you to choose from:

▶ making a chart or table

▶ writing a list

▶ drawing a picture

▶ taking a photograph

▶ keeping notes while you are working

▶ making a tape recording

▶ using a computer fact file

▶ writing about what you have done

1 GOING BAD

There are germs around us all the time. Most of the foods we eat have harmless germs in them but if we leave food for too long these germs can grow and spread. This makes the food go bad. The best places for germs to grow and spread are warm and damp. Can you say why it is not a good idea to touch bad food?

Warm, damp places

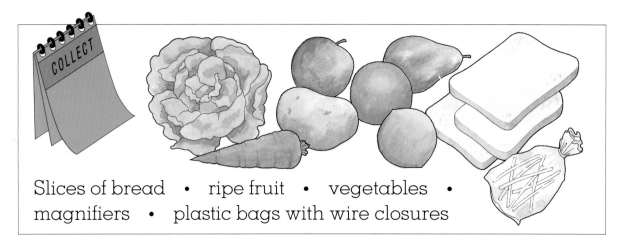

Slices of bread • ripe fruit • vegetables • magnifiers • plastic bags with wire closures

Look carefully at the foods you have collected. Put each kind of food into a plastic bag with a few drops of water. Close the bag tightly and put it in a warm place. You might use a sunny window sill or near a heater. Look at each bag every day but don't open it.

Make a diary to show the changes that you see every day.

How does it change?

	bread	apple	banana
Monday			
Tuesday	curling at edges	going brown softer	brown edges
Wednesday	Hard in middle dry	very brown wrinkles squeezy	squashy brown dark skin
Thursday	dark spots hard curly edges	brown very wrinkly rubber	black skin brown middle very squashy
Friday	mouldy patches hard edges	brown all over rubber	black skin very squashy brown.

Which food starts to go bad first? How can you tell?
How long does it take for each kind of food to go bad?

6

Keeping food for a long time

Frozen, tinned, fresh and dried peas • plastic bags

Sometimes food is frozen, put into tins or dried to keep it fresh. Look at the foods you have. What could stop germs growing? Open the packets and look again. Can you plan an investigation to find out which food will stay fresh longest now? Talk to your teacher about your plan. Make a list of the kinds of foods you have used. Next to each one write if you think it will go bad quickly or slowly and why. Watch each bag carefully. Which of your samples stays fresh the longest? Why?

Can you plan an investigation to find out if wet or dry food goes bad first? Can you use the results of your test to tell someone how to make their *compost* rot down quickly?

2 RUST

Some metal things change when they get damp.
Iron and sometimes steel will go rusty if it gets wet
and is then left in the air.

What makes things rust the quickest?

COLLECT

Iron filings •
kitchen towel • salt • cooking oil • 3 small dishes

ACTIVITY
– A –

Can you find out if things go
rusty more quickly if they are
wet or dry?
Cut three pieces of kitchen
towel and put them into
separate dishes.
Leave one piece of paper dry.
Wet one piece but let any extra
water run off. Cover one piece
with water. Sprinkle some iron
filings onto each piece of paper.
Leave them for 1 hour.

Look at the filings in the three dishes. What do you notice?
What does this tell you about rusting?
Write about the differences you can see.

ACTIVITY – B –

Cut 5 pieces of kitchen towel and put them in dishes. Label the dishes like this:

paper wet with warm water.

paper wet with cold water.

paper covered with cooking oil.

paper wet with salty water.

dry paper.

Make sure that the wet papers are just damp.
Sprinkle iron filings on top of each one. Look at the filings every 15 minutes. Note down any changes that you see.
Which filings rust first? Can you say why this is?
Which are the slowest to rust? Why?

RECORD

How will you show what you find out?

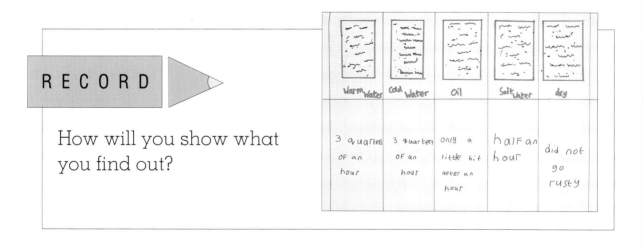

Warm water	Cold water	Oil	Salt water	dry
3 quarters of an hour	3 quarters of an hour	only a little bit after an hour	half an hour	did not go rusty

OTHER IDEAS

Can you use what you have found out to:
▶ say why it is important to keep iron railings painted?
▶ say why cars at the seaside might rust quicker than other cars?

3 LOOKING AT RUBBISH

This picture shows what the streets of a town can look like when the rubbish is not collected.

Write a story about what it would be like to live here. What problems would there be? Think about smells, germs, insects and rats.

How much rubbish does your class make?

Keep a list of everything that you throw away in one day. Can you make a chart with your friends to show what is thrown away by your class in one day? This group has sorted their lists into different materials which they throw away. Look at their chart. Which material do they throw away most, and which least? Why might this be?

How will you sort your list?

Biodegradable and not biodegradable

Germs, moulds and other living things rot or decay some of the rubbish we use. This kind of rubbish is *biodegradable*. Things like bits of food, dead plants, paper and wood are all biodegradable.

Some of the things we use will not decay even if they are left on a rubbish dump for a very long time. These things are not biodegradable. Most plastics, glass, metal and china are not biodegradable.

ACTIVITY

Look at this pile of rubbish. Make two lists to show the things which are and are not biodegradable.

Scientists have worked hard to make some plastics biodegradable. Biodegradable plastics can be used to cover pills and to make plastic stitches for people's cuts. Why might these things need to be made of biodegradable plastics?

Some plastic bags are also made of biodegradable plastics. How would you persuade someone to use a biodegradable plastic bag?

4   BREAKING THINGS DOWN

When we eat food our teeth chew it into pieces. The pieces go into our stomachs. We have special chemicals called enzymes in our stomachs which help to break down the food into liquid.

Sometimes chemicals are put onto *compost* heaps to make plants rot more quickly. The chemicals break down the plants into tiny pieces which can be dug back into the soil.

When we wash our clothes we use soap powder to break down the dirt so that it washes out easily. Some soap powders and liquids are *biological*. Biological powders have chemicals to break down the dirt more quickly.

Finding out about washing powders

Hard boiled egg   •
small, clear plastic pots   •   dishes   •   spoons   •
pieces of different foods (like bread, fruit and sugar)   •
biological and ordinary soap powders   •   rubber gloves

ACTIVITY – A –

Can you find out if biological powders help to break things down?

Remember to wear rubber gloves when you are working with soap powders.

Put a piece of egg into two jars. Add a spoonful of biological powder to one of the jars. Add a little warm water to each jar. Leave the jars in a warm place. Look at the jars at the end of the day and the next day.
Can you see any differences between the egg in the jars? Use a spoon to put the pieces of egg onto a dish. What do you notice now? Can you say why this has happened?

ACTIVITY – B –

Can you plan your own investigation?
You could try to find out:
▶ what happens to different foods in biological soap powder
▶ if ordinary soap powder breaks food down quicker than biological soap powder
▶ or your own ideas.
What will you do? What will you use?

RECORD

How will you make your record?

5 CHANGING WASTE

We throw away lots of materials which are not *biodegradable*. Why do you think this makes problems for us?

Some of the materials that we throw away can be used again to make new things. Old metal things like drink cans can be melted down to make new metal things. Used glass can be melted with a very hot flame and used to make new glass bottles. Used paper can be chopped or mashed up and mixed with water to make new paper. Things that are changed and used again are called recycled things.

These paper things have all been made from recycled paper. Can you tell that they are made from recycled paper?

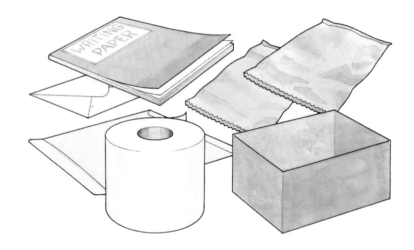

ACTIVITY

Can you collect some pieces of recycled paper? How do they look and feel different from other paper?
Can you think about ways that paper might be wasted at your school? Can you write some rules for saving paper?

Making recycled paper

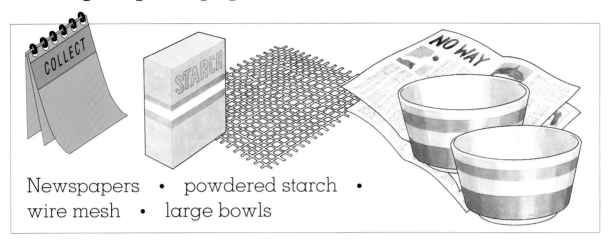

Newspapers • powdered starch • wire mesh • large bowls

1 Tear the newspaper into small pieces in a large bowl and cover them with water.

2 Leave them to soak. Stir them everyday for one week. Mix in some powdered starch.

3 Spread the wire over a bowl and tip your paper mix on top of it. Spread it out thinly and leave it to dry for one day.

4 Spread out some newspaper and carefully turn your wire on top of it.

5 Put more newspaper on top with a board or other flat weights.

6 Leave it for a few days until it is dry. Carefully peel the newspaper off and you should have a piece of recycled paper.

Things made from recycled paper are often more expensive than other paper things. Can you think why this is? Why might people not mind paying more to use recycled paper?

6 USING MATERIALS

There are already over 400 million cars in the world.
Imagine how big the scrapyard would have to be to hold
all those cars. Cars do not last forever because they
have metal body parts which rust. Can you say why
the body parts are made of metal?

Different materials are used to make cars

How would you persuade
people to buy a car with plastic
body parts? Think about what
might worry them about plastic
if they were used to owning a
car with metal body parts.
What would you need to tell
them? Write or draw an advertisement for your car.

Sometimes parts from old cars that still work are
saved to be used again. Other parts can be recycled.
The metal can be melted down and used again and the
rubber from the tyres can be used to make new tyres.
Can you see anything else which might be recycled?

metal parts

plastic parts

Melting to recycle

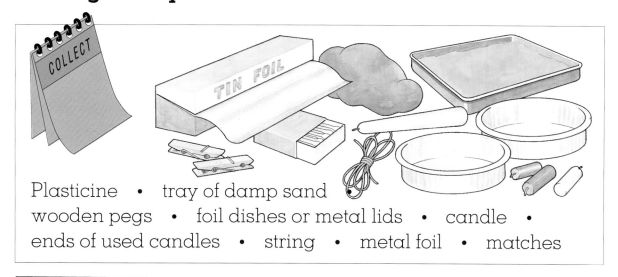

COLLECT

Plasticine • tray of damp sand
wooden pegs • foil dishes or metal lids • candle •
ends of used candles • string • metal foil • matches

ACTIVITY   Melting wax.

Remember to ask an adult to work with you
when using the lighted candle.

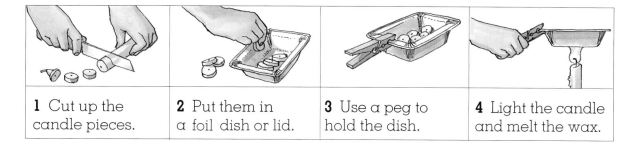

| **1** Cut up the candle pieces. | **2** Put them in a foil dish or lid. | **3** Use a peg to hold the dish. | **4** Light the candle and melt the wax. |

How does the wax change? How long does it take
to go hard again?

You can make some candle shapes for your melted wax.

| **1** Make your shape. | **2** Light the candle and melt the wax. | **3** Make a wick with some string. | **4** Fill your shape with wax. |

How are your recycled candles different from the other candles?

7 MELTING THINGS

We melt some foods when we are cooking. Which of these foods would melt if you heated them?

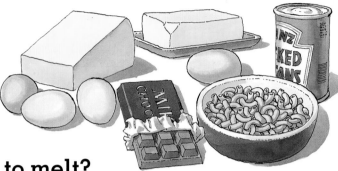

How long does it take to melt?

Margarine • butter • cheese • chocolate • timer • bun tray • oven gloves • a warm oven

    Remember to use oven gloves with hot things.

ACTIVITY

These children have heated a bun tray in an oven. They have put some of each food on the hot tray to see which melts first.
What will you do?
What will you use?
Will you need to use the same amount of each food? How could you measure?

How will you time how long each food takes to melt?
Try your test. Write about what you found out.

How hot does it need to get?

COLLECT

Foods which will melt • a kettle • thermometers •
dishes • jugs • your own ideas

ACTIVITY

Can you plan a test to find out how hot different
foods need to get before they melt?
Look at the foods that you have collected. Write
down which things you think would melt at a
low temperature and which at a higher
temperature? Talk to your teacher about your
plan.

These children have put some
warm water in a jug and
taken the temperature of the
water. They have put a dish
with some butter in it into the
water and watched to see
if the butter melts.
If the butter doesn't melt they
have carefully added more
hot water and taken the
temperature each time.

Look at the chart they
have made. At what
temperature did the butter
start to melt?

We used	melts at
☐ butter	55 °C
☑ cheese	70 °C
⊞ chocolate	75 °C
☐ jelly	70 °C
○ margarine	50 °C

Try out your test. Were your guesses right?

8 CHANGES IN COOKING

1 Shortcrust pastry

200g plain flour
pinch of salt
100g margarine
45ml water

Method:
1. Cut the margarine into pieces and rub in the flour and salt.
2. Mix water to make a stiff dough.
3. Roll out on a floured board.

2 Puff pastry

200g plain flour
1/2 teaspoon salt
130ml water
200g margarine

Method:
1. Mix flour, salt and water into a dough.
2. Roll into a rectangle, put the margarine in the middle of the dough and fold the edges over.
3. Roll the dough on a floured board and fold up again. Press the edges down.
4. Put the dough in a plastic bag and leave it in a fridge for 10 minutes.
5. Do this three times.

3 Choux pastry

65g plain flour
pinch of salt
50g margarine
100ml water
2 eggs
1 egg yolk

Method:
1. Put the margarine into the water and heat.
2. Take off heat and add flour.
3. Mix well and cool.
4. Beat in eggs, one at a time.
5. Add the egg yolk.

ACTIVITY

Look at these different pastry recipes.

Make a chart like the one here to show which ingredients are used in all the recipes and which are only used in some of them.

things which are used in all the pastry:	things which are only used in some:
flour	eggs
salt	sugar
marge	
water	

Making pastry

Ingredients and equipment for the recipes • baking trays

Wash your hands before touching food.
Use the recipes to make the different kinds
of pastry.
Look at the uncooked pastries. Do they look the
same or different? Do they smell the same?

Make some shapes using
the different kinds of pastry.
Put the pastry shapes on
baking trays and cook them
until they brown.
Look at the cooked pastry
shapes. How have they
changed in cooking? Did the
different types of pastry
take the same time to cook?
What do they feel like?
Do they smell and taste the
same?

RECORD How will you record what you find out?

9 MIXING THINGS

What happens when we mix things?

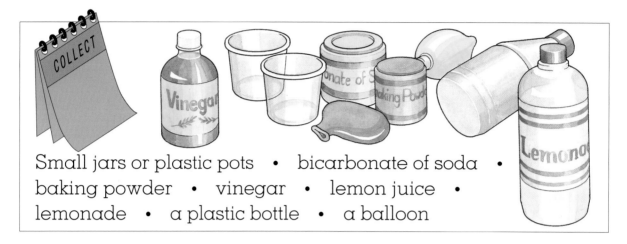

COLLECT

Small jars or plastic pots • bicarbonate of soda •
baking powder • vinegar • lemon juice •
lemonade • a plastic bottle • a balloon

Some things change each other when they are mixed together. Put a teaspoon of bicarbonate of soda into one of the jars. Add a tablespoon of water and watch what happens. Now put a teaspoon of bicarbonate of soda into another jar and add a tablespoon of vinegar. What happens this time?

Can you make some mixtures to find out which:
▶ makes most or least bubbles?
▶ bubbles longest?

ACTIVITY – A –

When you mix vinegar with bicarbonate of soda they make a gas. The gas escapes by pushing up bubbles. You can find out how strong this gas is. Go outside on a nice day with the things you have collected. Put some bicarbonate of soda in the bottle. Add some vinegar. Pull the balloon neck over the top of the bottle. What happens? Why?

Can you find out why we sometimes use bicarbonate of soda or baking powder in cooking? Collect the ingredients and equipment you will need for this recipe.

Scones

200g self-raising flour
50g margarine
7 tablespoons milk

Mix the ingredients like this:

Roll out the three mixes and cut out some scones.
Put the scones on baking trays and put them in a hot oven.
When the scones are cooked get them out and leave them to cool.

Remember to use oven gloves when touching hot things.

Look at your scones. Do they all look, feel, smell and taste the same?
Can you write about how the bicarbonate of soda and baking powder changed the scones?

10 CHANGING THINGS

Using indicators to change colours

Small plastic pots • sticky labels • red cabbage • pan • hot ring • vinegar • a collection of liquids (like lemonade, lemon juice, soda water, orange juice, tea) • spoons • bicarbonate of soda

Lots of the things we use are *acids*, like lemon juice. To find out which things are acids we can use an indicator which is turned pink or red by acid things. Make some indicator like this:

Put cabbage into a saucepan

add water

heat then cool

drain off the water

Put a teaspoon of bicarbonate of soda in one pot and a teaspoon of lemon juice in another. Add a little of your indicator to each pot. Which one is the acid?

ACTIVITY – B –

Can you use your indicator to find out which other liquids are acids?

Try putting some other liquids into pots. For each one say if you think it is an acid before you add the indicator.

Think about a way to show:
▶ what you tested
▶ what colour you thought it would go
▶ and the colour it went.
Try your tests. Which ones surprised you?

The liquids which turned the indicator green are alkalis.
If the indicator stayed purple the liquids were *neutral*.

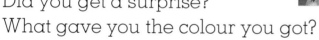

Mix a teaspoon of acid with a
teaspoon of alkali. What do you
think will happen when you
add some indicator? Why?
Try and see what happens.
Did you get a surprise?
What gave you the colour you got?

Can you investigate how much alkali it takes to make
an acid neutral?
How will you know that you have made the acid neutral?
What will you use? How will you measure?

Write about what you did and what
you found out.

When we have too much acid in our stomachs
we get indigestion. Can you plan a test to find
out which indigestion tablets work the best?

11 FREEZING THINGS

Freezing liquids

Small clear plastic pots • marker pens •
a freezer • different liquids (like milk,
lemonade, orange, cola, water and salty water)

Things can be changed by
heating. They can be changed
by cooling too.
Use one pot for each different
liquid. Put some of each liquid
in the pots and mark how high
it comes up to on the side of the
pot.

Put the pots in the freezer and leave them. Look at the
pots every 30 minutes until all the liquids have frozen.
How have the liquids changed?
Can you draw each pot and write under each one how
the liquids have changed?

Can you investigate:
▶   how long each pot takes to *thaw*?
▶   What happens to each liquid?

Keeping and melting ice cubes

Ice cubes in a vacuum flask •
timers • your own ideas

ACTIVITY Fold a piece of paper in half. On one half write down ways of keeping an ice cube cold. On the other half write down ways of melting an ice cube quickly. Think of as many ways as you can.

Look at your lists. Choose one way from each side to test. Why did you choose these ways?
Plan your test and try your ways.
How long did you manage to keep an ice cube?
How quickly could you make an ice cube melt?
Can you make a class chart to help you find the best way of melting and keeping ice cubes?

ice cubes	
melting	Keeping
under tap	put in fridge
in mouth	in sawdust
rub in hands	in cotten wool
on heater	in polystyme
in oven	chips
	in sand

Can you say how you would keep frozen food cold on a long journey?

12 STOPPING CHANGES

The things that people do often change the Earth.
Some things spoil the places where we live.
How might these things spoil the Earth?

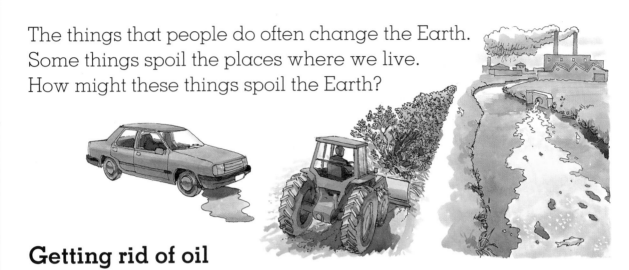

Getting rid of oil

Clear or white water tray • food colouring •
cooking oil • your own ideas

ACTIVITY

Put some water into the tray
and add food colouring to
make coloured water.
This will help you to see
what is happening. Pour
some oil on the water.
What happens? What does it look like?

Can you think of some ways to try to get rid of the oil?
Try some of your ways. Do they work?
Write about the ways you tried and how well they worked.

When lots of oil is spilt onto the sea we call it an oil slick. Can you find out how people try to clean up real oil slicks?

Spoiling the land

Pots of soil • cress seeds • your own ideas

Write or draw a list of ways that the land could be spoiled.

Plant some cress seeds in each pot and think about how you could spoil the soil in your pots. Why is it a good idea to keep one pot unspoilt? Label your pots.

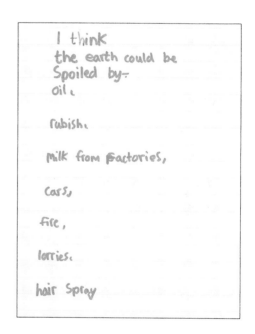

I think the earth could be Spoiled by—
oil.

rubish.

milk from factories,

cars,

fire,

lorries.

hair Spray

Can you investigate to find out:
▶ which of your ideas stops plants growing?
▶ if the plants will grow when you stop spoiling the soil?

R E C O R D ▷ Find a way to show your results.

13 POLLUTION

When we spoil the land, air or water we make the
Earth a less safe place to live in. This is called pollution.
What sorts of things are polluting these places?

Investigating pollution from roads

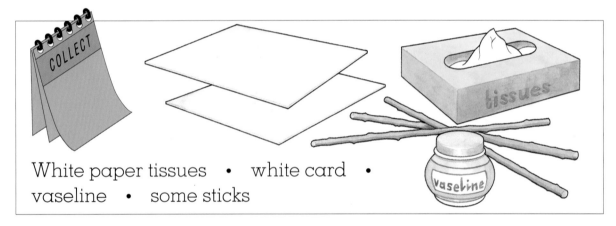

White paper tissues • white card •
vaseline • some sticks

ACTIVITY
– A –

Can you find out what happens
to the plants near a road?
Ask a grown-up to help you.
Take a white paper tissue and
wipe the leaves of some plants
growing near a road. Look at
the tissue. What do you see?

Take another tissue and do the same thing with some plants growing away from a road. What do you notice?
What could have made a difference?

Why do you think that these houses look dirty?

ACTIVITY – B –
Make some pollution detectors like these.

Choose some places to put them. Choose some places where you think there will be lots of pollution and some where you think there will not. Look at them each day. Can you see where most pollution happens?

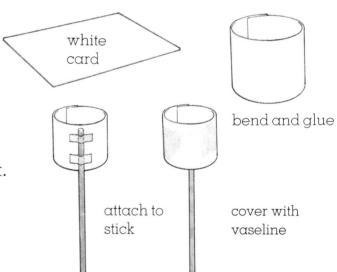

white card

bend and glue

attach to stick

cover with vaseline

RECORD ▷ Make a chart to show your results. Where did you get most pollution? Why?

FIND OUT Can you find out how scientists have tried to make pollution from cars less dangerous?

14 HARMING OURSELVES

Some of the jobs which people do could harm their bodies.
We breathe air into our lungs. If the air has a lot
of dust in it then the dust goes into our lungs as well.

People who work with a lot of dust wear special masks to
let the air through but keep the dust out. Why might
the workers in these pictures need masks?

Keeping dust out

Coloured powder paint • yoghurt pots •
rubber bands • scissors • white paper •
a collection of different materials

 Can you test to find which materials will keep
most dust out? Remember that these
special masks must let air in.

Put some powder paint in each yoghurt pot.
Choose some materials which you think will
keep the "dust" in your pots. Write down
which materials you are using and
why you chose them.
Cover each pot with one
of your materials and
shake them over a piece
of white paper.

How will you show what you find out?
Which material would you tell a builder to use for a mask? Why?

Keeping healthy

Can you find out about things which are bad
for your body? Some children have made this
game. If you land on a square which has
something which keeps your body healthy then
you go up a ladder.
If you land on a square which has something
which harms your body you go down a snake.
Can you make a game?

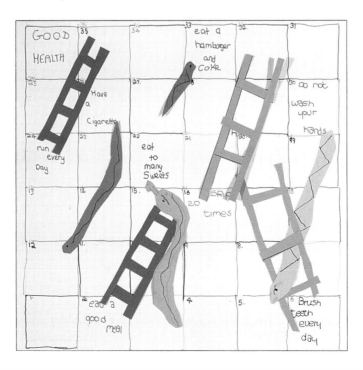

15   LOOKING AT TEETH

When we are born we do not have any teeth which show. Can you find out how old most babies are when their teeth start to show? When children are about six or seven years old they start to lose their first teeth and grow a new set.

These teeth should last them for the rest of their lives so it is important that they look after these teeth.

These drawings show the top set of an adult's teeth.

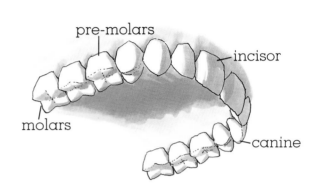

pre-molars

incisor

molars

canine

Making an impression of your teeth

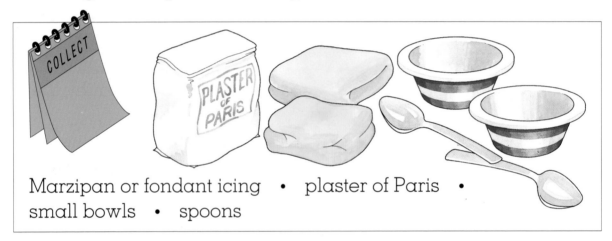

Marzipan or fondant icing • plaster of Paris •
small bowls • spoons

ACTIVITY

You can make an impression of your top teeth. Bite into the marzipan. Fill the marzipan mould with plaster of Paris. Let it dry and peel off the marzipan.

How do we keep our teeth healthy?

Can you draw or write a list of things which you should do to keep your teeth healthy?
Some children have made a chart to show how many times a day the children in their class clean their teeth.
How many times a day do you clean your teeth?

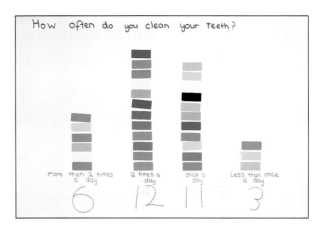

How often do you clean your teeth?

| more than 2 times a day | 2 times a day | once a day | Less than once a day |
| 6 | 12 | 11 | 3 |

Teeth are hard to clean because little bits of food can get inside the gaps between them. When you brush your teeth do you brush from side to side, up and down or both ways? Can you plan a test to find out which way is best?
These children have rubbed black paint onto some lolly sticks.
They are giving each set five brushes with the toothbrush.
Do you think their test is fair?
What will you use to help you test?

RECORD ▷ How will you show what you find out?

16   HEALTHY EATING

It is important that our bodies get enough to eat.
It is also important that we eat the right kinds of food.
We eat different kinds of food:

Proteins like these help
our bodies to grow
and keep strong.

Carbohydrates like
these help to give
our bodies energy.

These foods have lots of
minerals and vitamins
in them to help to
keep our bodies healthy.

If we eat some of these kinds of foods every day we have
a healthy diet. We call it a balanced diet.

ACTIVITY
– A –

These children are
holding cards to
show what they
have eaten today.
Have they all had a
balanced diet? Can
you say what they
should eat to make
their diets balanced?

Can you plan a balanced meal and make a menu card for these children?

Sophie is a vegetarian. She doesn't eat meat or fish.
Sadia wants a packed lunch for school.
Arnold has come home for tea after going swimming.

Soaking up water

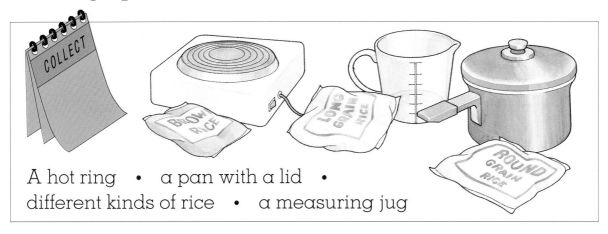

COLLECT

A hot ring • a pan with a lid •
different kinds of rice • a measuring jug

ACTIVITY

Our bodies need water or they would dry out.
We get water from drinks and in some food.
Sometimes we add water in cooking. Foods like
rice soak up water when they are cooked.
Can you investigate how much water different
kinds of rice soak up when they are cooked?

You need a grown-up to help you. Remember to
be careful with hot water.

Boil 4 cups of water in a pan.
Add 1 cup of rice. Put the lid on.
Cook the rice gently until it is
fluffy. Take it off the heat to cool
on a mat. Find out how much
water is left. Can you find out if
other kinds of rice soak up more
or less water?

17 CHANGING LIGHT

We use light in lots of ways. Sometimes we use coloured and flashing lights. Can you think of some places where coloured and flashing lights are used? Here are some pictures to start you thinking.

Why do you think flashing lights are useful?

Changing light in different ways

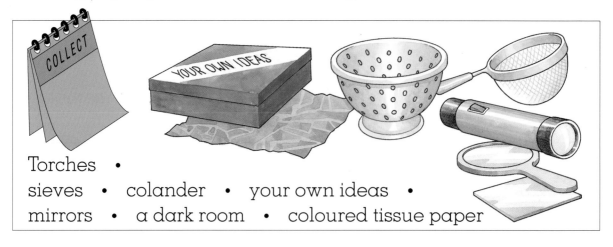

Torches •
sieves • colander • your own ideas •
mirrors • a dark room • coloured tissue paper

ACTIVITY – A – Can you use your torch to make different coloured lights? Does it work well?
What happens when you mix two different coloured lights?

ACTIVITY – B –

Try using the torches with sieves, colanders and other things with holes in to make light patterns.

ACTIVITY – C –

Shine the torch onto a wall. Does the light go straight to the wall? How can you find out? Can you find out if light always travels in straight lines?

These children are trying to make light change direction. What are they doing? Why do you think they are trying these ways?

Try some of their ideas and some of your own.

RECORD ▷ Remember to keep notes or drawings to show what you tried and what happened. Which way is best?

18   SHADOWS

How does light travel?

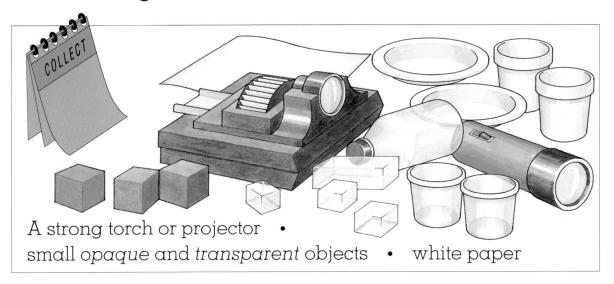

A strong torch or projector   •
small *opaque* and *transparent* objects   •   white paper

ACTIVITY – A – What happens when light meets something which it cannot travel through?
Shine the light onto the white paper.

Does it go in a straight line?
Now hold your hand between the light and the piece of paper.
What happens to the light?
When light cannot go through something, it cannot go round it so a shadow is made.

Try holding different things between the light and the paper.
Why do you think you get different sizes and shapes of shadows?

ACTIVITY – B – Hold something which makes a shadow in front of your light. Hold it still and ask someone to move the light nearer. What happens to the shadow? What might happen if the light was moved further away? Try it and see.

Transparent things like glass let the light through. Try holding some transparent things in front of your light. What do you see? Can you see a faint shadow? Why do you think you can see this?

Look at this photograph.

These children are trying to find out why the footballers have more than one shadow.

OTHER IDEAS

Can you make a shadow puppet theatre and make up a play for your friends?

19 CHANGING COLOURS

Before people had *dyes* most of their clothes would have been the colour of the animal skins or wool used to make them. The first dyes which people used were made from plants growing where they lived. They learned how to boil the plants to make different colours. Today chemical dyes are used to colour our clothes.

Making dyes from plants

Some plants (like onions, leaves, red cabbage) • pans • hot ring • a piece of white cloth cut into squares • washing soda • vinegar • wooden tongs or pegs • salt • candles • string • your own ideas

  Remember to ask a grown-up before you pick plants.

 Look at the plants you have.
Draw the plants and next to each one write or colour to show which colour dye it might make.

  Remember to be careful with hot water. Ask a grown-up to help.

Use the plants to make dye like this. Put one kind of plant into a saucepan of water. Heat it gently then let it cool.

Using tongs or pegs dip a piece of cloth into each dye. Which colours do you get? Can you make a shade chart like this one?

Shade chart

onions   Cabbage
                    nettles
     Cabbage +
     Lemon
Cabbage   Lime
+ soda

ACTIVITY
– B –

If dyes are not fixed they will come out when the cloth is washed.
Salt is sometimes used to fix dyes.
Can you plan an investigation to find out if salt helps to fix your dyes? What will you do?
How will you show what you find out?
What else could you try?

ACTIVITY
– C –

You can make patterns on your cloth in different ways. Here are some ways you could try:

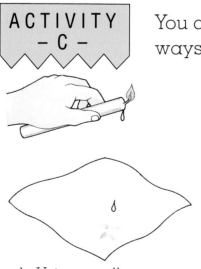

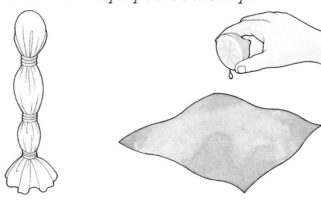

1 Using candle wax   2 Tying it with string   3 Using lemon juice

20 DETECTIVE GAMES

Can you see it?

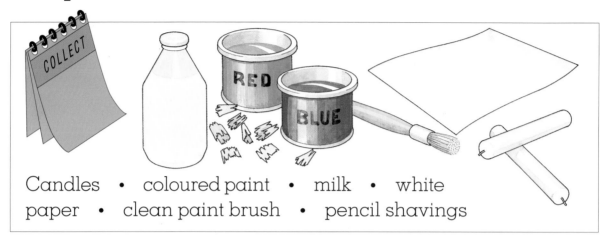

Candles • coloured paint • milk • white
paper • clean paint brush • pencil shavings

ACTIVITY
– A –

Use a white candle to draw
a picture on a white piece
of paper.
Can you see your picture?
Can you make your picture
appear?
Try painting over the paper
with watery paint.
Can you see the picture
now?
Why does the picture show
now?

ACTIVITY
– B –

Use a paint brush and some milk to paint a
picture. Let the picture dry. When it is dry rub
pencil shavings over it. What do you notice?

Can you investigate to find out if anything else
makes the milk show up?

Invisible ink

Paper • paint brush • onion • lemon or orange juice • an iron or oven

Prisoners in the Second World War learnt that they could write secret messages with invisible ink. The messages would appear when the paper was heated enough to burn the ink but not the paper.

Remember to be careful with hot things.

Use the fruit juice to paint a picture on the paper.
Can you see the picture?
Cover your picture with another piece of paper.
Now iron the paper with a cool iron or put it in a cool oven (100 °C) for 10 minutes.
What happens?
Why does this happen?

Try using other things to make invisible writing.
You could try onion juice or your own ideas.

Glossary

Acid

There are lots of different kinds of acids, some are used in the cleaners that we have at home or school. Acidic food or drinks taste sharp or sour.

Biodegradable

Germs, moulds and other living things rot or decay biodegradable things.

Biological

Biological washing powders have special chemicals in them which help to get rid of stains like blood or grass from our clothes.

Compost

Compost is a mixture of decaying plants which can be added to soil to help plants to grow.

Dyes

Dyes are used to change the colour of cloth. They can also be used to change the colour of hair.

Neutral

If something is neutral, it is neither acid or alkaline.

Opaque

If something is opaque, you cannot see through it. A wooden door is opaque.

Thaw

When something that is frozen thaws, it melts or softens.

Transparent

If something is transparent, you can see through it. Water and clear glass are transparent.

Index